T0105189

the LAUGH GIRAFFE

350 Hilarious Jokes!

Sky Pony Press
New York

Sky Pony Press books may be purchased in bulk at special discounts for sales promotion, corporate gifts, fund-raising, or educational purposes. Special editions can also be created to specifications. For details, contact the Special Sales Department, Sky Pony Press, 307 West 36th Street, 11th Floor, New York, NY 10018 or info@skyhorsepublishing.com.

Sky Pony® is a registered trademark of Skyhorse Publishing, Inc.®, a Delaware corporation.

Visit our website at www.skyponypress.com.

10 9 8 7 6 5 4 3 2 1

Manufactured in China, 2020

This product conforms to CPSIA 2008

Library of Congress Cataloging-in-Publication Data is available on file.

ISBN: 978-1-5107-5839-1
EISBN: 978-1-5107-5840-7

Cover design by Daniel Brount
Illustrations by Alex Paterson

Printed in China

Table of Contents

"What?" Jokes

What dog keeps the best time?

A watch dog!

☆

What did the traffic light say to the car?

Don't look, I'm changing!

☆

What word looks the same backwards and upside down?

S W I M S!

☆

What did the spider do on the computer?

Made a web site!

☆

What is brown and has a head and
a tail but no legs?

A penny!

☆

What did the penny say to the
other penny?

We make perfect cents!

☆

What sound do porcupines make
when they kiss?

"Ouch!"

☆

What did the singer do when he locked himself out?

He sang until he found the right key!

☆

What is the best day to go to the beach?

Any Sunday!

☆

What stays on the ground but never gets dirty?

A shadow!

☆

What goes up and down but does not move?

Stairs!

☆

What goes up when the rain comes down?

An umbrellla!

"What?" Jokes

What's taken before you get it?

A picture!

☆

What did the sink say to the toilet?

You look really flushed!

☆

What do you do with a sick boat?

Take it to the doc!

☆

What can you catch but not throw?

A cold!

☆

What is the most hardworking part of the eye?

The pupil!

☆

What do prisoners use to call each other?

Cell phones!

☆

What kind of button doesn't unbutton?

A belly button!

☆

What nails do carpenters hate to hit?

Fingernails!

☆

"What?" Jokes

What washes up on very small beaches?

Microwaves!

☆

What is heavy forwards but NOT backwards?

Ton!

☆

What do cannon balls do when they're in love?

Make bb's!

☆

What kind of key opens a banana?

A mon-key!

☆

What stays in a corner and travels all over the world?

A stamp!

What did one elevator say to the other elevator?

I think I'm coming down with something!

What has four wheels and flies?

A garbage truck!

What color is the wind?

Blew!

What music scares balloons?

Pop music!

☆

What can you find once in a minute, twice in a moment, but never in a year?

The letter M!

☆

What is red and smells like blue paint?

Red paint!

☆

What's brown and sticky?

A stick!

☆

What's red and goes up and down?

A tomato in an elevator!

What kind of room doesn't have doors?

A mushroom!

☆

What kind of shoes do frogs wear?

Open toad!

☆

What did one snowman say to the other?

Do you smell carrots?

☆

What do you get from a pampered cow?

Spoiled milk!

☆

What bow can't be tied?

A rainbow!

☆

What happens to a frog's car when it breaks down?

It gets toad!

☆

What do you use to count cows?

A cow-culator!

☆

What do computers eat for a snack?

Microchips!

☆

What did the hamburger name his daughter?

Patty!

☆

What do lawyers wear to court?

Law suits!

☆

What did the buffalo say when his boy went to school?

Bison!

☆

What gets wetter the more it dries?

A towel!

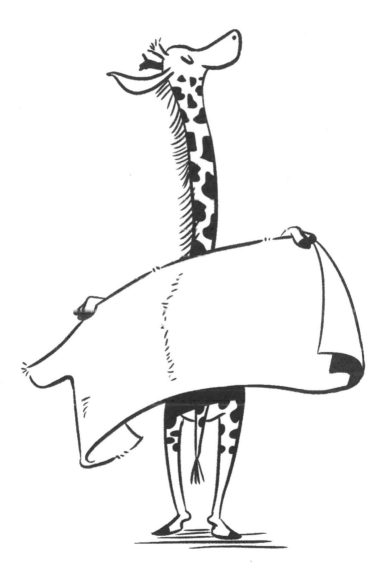

What runs but stays in the same place?

A refrigerator!

☆

What falls and never gets hurt?

Rain!

☆

What did the blanket say to the bed?

Don't worry. I've got you covered!

☆

What word starts with E and ends with E and has one letter in it?

Envelope!

☆

"What?" Jokes

What is it that even the most
careful person overlooks?

His nose!

What did one eye say to the other
eye?

Between us, something smells!

What runs but can't walk?

A faucet!

What has one horn and gives
milk?

A milk truck!

"Why?" Jokes

Why don't cannibals eat clowns?

Because they taste funny!

☆

Why couldn't the bike stand up?

Because it was two tired!

☆

Why didn't the skeleton go to the party?

He had no body to go with!

☆

Why did the cookie go to the doctor?

Because it felt crummy!

☆

Why did the banana go to the doctor?

Because it wasn't peeling well!

Why couldn't the pony sing a song?

Because it was a little horse!

Why did the boy tiptoe past the medicine cabinet?

Because he didn't want to wake the sleeping pills!

Why was the tomato red?

Because it saw the salad dressing!

Why do watermelons have big weddings?

Because they cantaloupe!

☆

Why did the scarecrow win a Nobel prize?

Because it was outstanding in it's field!

☆

Why can't a leopard hide?

Because he's always spotted!

☆

Why did the student eat his homework?

Because the teacher said it was a piece of cake!

☆

Why did the boy throw the clock

out the window?

Because he wanted to see time fly!

Why was the math book sad?

Because it had too many problems!

☆

Why couldn't the astronaut get a hotel room on the moon?

Because it was full!

☆

Why did the Teddy bear say no to dessert?

Because he was stuffed!

☆

Why is there a fence around cemeteries?

Because people are dying to get in!

☆

Why aren't dogs good dancers?

Because they have two left feet!

Why do bagpipers walk when they play?

To gct away from the noise!

Why did the bird go to the hospital?

To get a tweet-ment!

Why did the man put his money in the freezer?

He wanted cold hard cash!

Why did the girl bring a ladder to school?

Because it was a high school!

Why does the chicken coop have only two doors?

Because if it had four doors it would be a chicken sedan!

☆

Why are ghosts bad liars?

Because you can see right through them!

☆

Why do scuba divers fall backwards out of a boat?

Because if the fell forwards, they'd fall into the boat!

☆

Why did the picture go to jail?

Because it was framed!

☆

Why can't you tell a kleptomaniac a joke?

Because they take things, literally!

☆

Why did the woman become an archaeologist?

Because her career was in ruins!

☆

Why did the baby strawberry cry?

Because his parents were in a jam!

☆

Why did the man put a clock under his desk?

Because he wanted to work over time!

☆

"Why?" Jokes

Why was 6 afraid of 7!

Because 7 ate 9!

☆

Why did 7 eat 9?

Because you're supposed to eat 3
squared meals a day!

☆

**Why did the old man fall into the
well?**

Because he couldn't see that well!

☆

**Why did the banana lose his
driver's license?**

Because he peeled out!

☆

Why isn't there a clock in the library?

Because it tocks too much!

Why did the soccer player bring string to the game?

So he could tie the score!

☆

Why couldn't the lifeguard save the hippie?

Because he was too far out!

☆

Why did the fungus leave the fungi?

There was not mushroom!

☆

Why can't you hear a pterodactyl go to the bathroom?

Because the P is silent!

Why are robots never afraid?

Because they have nerves of steel!

Why did the mushroom go to the party?

Because he was a fungi!

☆

Why did the teacher wear sunglasses?

Because her students were so bright!

☆

Why didn't the koala bear get the job?

Because it was over koala-fied!

☆

Why couldn't the sailors play cards?

Because the captain was sitting on the deck!

☆

Why do geese fly south in the
winter?

It's too far to walk!

☆

Why do flamingos always lift one
leg while standing?

Because if they lifted two legs
they'd fall down!

☆

Why did the computer go to the
doctor?

Because it had a virus!

☆

Why don't seagulls live by the
bay?

Because then they'd be bagels!

☆

Why is basketball a messy sport?

Because you dribble on the floor!

☆

Why was Dracula put in jail?

He tried to rob a blood bank!

☆

Why did the baker get arrested?

For beating the eggs!

☆

Why did the robber take a bath?

Because he wanted to make a clean getaway!

☆

Why can't you tell a secret to a burrito?

Because they tend to spill the beans!

☆

Why was the broom late for school?

It over swept!

☆

Why do sharks only swim in salt water?

Because pepper makes them sneeze!

☆

Why is Santa so good at karate?

Because he has a black belt!

☆

Why do you never see elephants hiding in trees?

Because they are very good at it!

"What Do You Get When?" Jokes

What do you get when you cross a

bank and a skunk?

Dollars and scents!

☆

What do you get when you cross

50 female pigs and 50 male

deer?

100 sows and bucks!

☆

What do you get when you cross a

porcupine and a baby goat?

A stuck-up kid!

☆

What do you get when you cross a

fly, a rug, a car, and a cat?

A flying car-pet!

☆

What do you get when you cross a lemon and a cat?

A sourpuss!

☆

What do you get when you cross a dinosaur and a termite?

Dino-mite!

☆

What do you get when you cross an elephant and a kangaroo?

Big holes in the ground!

☆

What do you get when you cross an elephant and a cat?

A flat cat!

☆

What do you get when you cross and elephant and a potato?

Mashed potatoes!

☆

What do you get when you cross an elephant and a sports car?

A car with a big trunk!

☆

What do you get when you cross a bear with a skunk?

Winnie the pee-yoo!

☆

What do you get when you cross a fish and an elephant?

Swimming trunks!

☆

What do you get when you cross a cobra and a porcupine?

Barbed wire!

☆

What do you get when you cross a turkey and an octopus?

Enough drumsticks for everyone!

☆

What do you get when you cross a cat and a parrot?

A carrot!

☆

What do you get when you cross a cat and Kris Kringle?

Santa Claws!

☆

What do you get when cross a cat
and a canary?

Shredded tweet!

☆

What do you get when you cross a
cat and a tree?

A cat-a-log!

☆

What do you get when you cross
strawberries with rush hour?

A traffic jam!

☆

What do you get when you cross a
dog and a hen?

Pooched eggs!

☆

What do you get when you cross a gorilla and a cat?

An animal that puts you out at night!

☆

What do you get when you cross a shark and an iceberg?

Frostbite!

☆

What do you get when you cross a hamburger and a computer?

A Big Mac!

☆

What do you get when you cross a parrot and a centipede?

A walkie talkie!

☆

What do you get when you cross a cat and a ghost?

A scaredy cat!

☆

What do you get when you cross a cocker spaniel, a poodle, and a rooster?

Cockapoodledoo!

☆

What do you get when you cross a giraffe and a hedgehog?

An 8-foot toothbrush!

"What Do You Get When?" Jokes

What do you get when you cross a snake with a kangaroo?

A jump rope!

☆

What do you get when you cross a panther and a hamburger?

Really fast food!

☆

What do you get when you cross a porcupine and a turtle?

A slow poke!

☆

What do you get when you cross a bell with a bat?

A dingbat!

☆

What do you get when you cross a rabbit and a frog?

A bunny ribbit!

☆

What do you get when you cross a trampoline and a cow?

A milkshake!

☆

What do you get when you cross a cow and a lawnmower?

A lawn-mooer!

☆

What do you get when you cross a story with the biggest mammal?

A whale of a tale!

☆

What do you get when you cross a Border Collie and a rose?

A collie-flower!

☆

"What Do You Call?" Jokes

What do you call a fake noodle?

An im-pasta!

☆

What do you call a meditating wolf?

Aware wolf!

☆

What do you call two birds in love?

Tweet-hearts!

☆

What do you call twin dinosaurs?

A pair-odactyls!

☆

What do you call dancing sheep?

Baa-larinas!

☆

What do you call a sad cup of coffee?

A despresso!

☆

What do you call a deer with a dollar?

A buck!

☆

What do you call a woman who catches fish?

Annette!

☆

What do you call a three-footed aardvark?

A yard-vark!

What do you call a man who's not religious?

God-frey!

What do you call a witch at the beach?

A sand-witch!

What do you call an illegally parked frog?

Toad!

What do you call an elephant that doesn't matter?

Ir-elephant!

☆

VAST,
ENORMOUS,
TITANIC,
SIZEABLE
GIGANTIC

What do you call a dinosaur with a big vocabulary?

A thesaurus!

☆

"What Do You Call?" Jokes

What do you call 50 rabbits in a row hopping backwards?

A receding hare-line!

What do you call a man with cat scratches?

Claude!

What do you call a man with a car on his head?

Jack!

What do you call a man who likes food seasonings?

Herb!

What do you call a deer with no eyes?

No eye-dear!

☆

What do you call a Jedi with one arm?

Hand Solo!

What do you call a skunk in a helicopter?

A smelly-copter!

☆

What do you call a bear in the rain?

A drizzly bear!

☆

What do you call a man with a crane?

Derek!

☆

What do you call a monkey that likes Doritos?

A chip-monk!

☆

What do you call a man with a map?

Miles!

☆

What do you call a boomerang that doesn't work?

A stick!

"What Do You Call?" Jokes

What do you call a person who doesn't fart in public?

A private toot-er!

☆

What do you call a Frenchman wearing sandals?

Phillipe Flop!

☆

What do you call a shaky cow?

Beef jerky!

☆

What do you call strawberries in a rock band?

A jam session!

☆

What do you call a woman with a sun lamp?

Tan-ya!

☆

What do you call a policeman in bed?

An undercover detective!

☆

What do you call a woman with a turtle?

Shelley!

☆

What do you call a cat that eats beans?

Puss 'n toots!

☆

What do you call killer whales
that play music?

An orca-stra!

☆

What do you call a man in a
mailbox?

Bill!

☆

What do you call a tiny mother?

A mini-mum!

☆

What do you call a priest who becomes a lawyer?

Father-in-law!

☆

What do you call a fish with no eyes?

Fsh!

☆

What do you call a woman with a cat?

Kitty!

☆

What do you call lending money to a bison?

A buffa-loan!

☆

What do you call a zebra with no stripes?

A horse!

☆

What do you call a cold poodle?

A chili-dog!

☆

What do you call a fly without wings?

A walk!

☆

What do you call a boy named Lee that no one talks to?

Lone-Lee!

☆

What do you call a cow with no legs?

Ground beef!

☆

What do you call a sleeping bull?

A bulldozer!

☆

What do you call birds that stick together?

Velcrows!

☆

What do you call a man flat on the floor?

Matt!

☆

What do you call a ten-foot-high stack of frogs?

A toad-em-pole!

☆

What do you call a pony with a sore throat?

A little hoarse!

☆

What do you call an argument between two electric companies?

A power struggle!

☆

What do you call a man with a shovel?

Doug!

☆

What do you call a man without a shovel?

Doug-less!

☆

What do you call a pile of cats?

A meow-tain!

☆

What do you call a burglar with a rubber toe?

Robber-toe!

☆

What do you call a man on his knees?

Neil!

☆

What do you call a flying bagel?

A plane bagel!

☆

What do you call a man with a toilet?

John!

☆

What do you call a sleepwalking nun?

A roamin' Catholic!

☆

What do you call cheese that doesn't belong to you?

Nacho cheese!

☆

What do you call it when a cow spies on a bull?

A steak-out!

☆

What do you call a belt with a watch on it?

A waist of time!

☆

What do you call a bear with no socks?

Bear foot!

☆

What do you call a smelly Santa?

Farter Christmas!

☆

What do you call a man hanging on a wall?

Art!

☆

What do you call a man with an elephant on his head?

An ambulance!

☆

"Cross the Road" Jokes

Why did the chicken cross the road?

To get to the other side!

☆

Why did the chewing gum cross the road?

Because it got stuck on the chicken's foot!

☆

Why did the giraffe cross the grasslands?

Because there weren't any roads nearby!

☆

Why didn't the chicken cross the road?

Because it got run over half-way across.

☆

Why did the redneck cross the road?

To eat the run-over chicken!

☆

Why did the duck cross the road?

Because the chicken had the day off!

☆

Why did the chicken cross the road?

Because it was free range!

☆

How did the dead chicken cross the road?

In a KFC bucket!

☆

Why did the chicken cross the road?

To get out of Kentucky!

☆

Why didn't the roast chicken cross the road?

It didn't have the guts any more!

☆

Why did the rooster cross the road?

To show he wasn't chicken!

☆

Why did the rubber chicken cross the road?

He wanted to stretch his legs!

☆

Why did the chicken cross the road?

Because the light was green!

☆

Why did the lettuce cross the road?

Because it was green!

☆

Why did the elephant cross the road?

To visit the chicken!

☆

Why were there feathers in the road?

Because the wolf got the chicken!

☆

Why did the reindeer cross the road?

Because he was tied to the chicken!

☆

Why did the chicken cross the road?

I'm sure it had its reasons!

☆

Why did the hen cross the road?

She thought it was an egg-cellent idea!

☆

"Cross the Road" Jokes

Why did the hippo cross the road?

To visit the elephant!

☆

Why did the chicken cross the road?

All of its friends were doing it!

☆

Why did the chicken cross the playground?

To get to the other slide!

☆

"Cross the Road" Jokes

Why did the dinosaur cross the road?

Because chickens hadn't been invented yet!

⭐

Why didn't the dinosaur cross the road?

Because roads hadn't been invented yet!

⭐

Why did the fish cross the ocean?

To get to the other tide!

⭐

Why didn't the bicycle cross the road?

Because it was two-tired!

⭐

"Cross the Road" Jokes

Why didn't the ghost cross the road?

It had no body to go with!

☆

Why did the one-armed man cross the road?

To go to the secondhand store!

☆

How did the egg cross the road?

He scrambled!

☆

Why did the potato run across the road?

Because it didn't want to be mashed!

☆

"Cross the Road" Jokes

Why did the baby skeleton cross the road?

To see its mummy!

☆

Why did the skeleton cross the road?

To go to the body shop!

☆

Why did the monkey cross the road?

Because the chicken retired!

☆

"Cross the Road" Jokes

Why was everyone mad at the pig crossing the road?

Because he was a road hog!

What happened when the elephant crossed the road?

He crushed the chicken!

Why did the cow cross the road?

To go to the moo-vies!

Why did the cow cross the road?

To get to the udder side!

Why couldn't the toilet paper cross the road?

Because it got stuck in a crack!

☆

Why did the baby chick cross the road with its mother?

Because it was take your child to work day!

☆

Why did the turtle cross the road?

To get to the Shell station!

☆

Why did the duck cross the road?

Because it thought it was a chicken!

☆

"Cross the Road" Jokes

Why did the fish cross the road?

To get to its school!

Why did the dog cross the road?

Because he was chasing the chicken!

Why did the chicken cross the basketball court?

Because the referee was calling fowls!

Why did the chicken cross the road, roll in dirt, and cross again?

Because he was a dirty double crosser!

Why did the nose cross the road?

It was tired of getting picked on!

☆

Why did the chicken cross the road?

To find a place where no one would question his intention of crossing a road!

☆

Why did the chicken cross the road?

It got tired of too many people making chicken jokes!

☆

"Did You Hear?" Jokes

Did you hear about the rich rabbit?

He was a million-hare!

Did you hear about the kidnapping?

He woke up!

Did you hear the vegetable joke?

It's corny!

Did you hear about the man who stole soap?

He made a clean getaway!

Did you hear about the musical ghost?

He wrote haunting melodies!

Did you hear about the boy who hated working on his father's farm so he went to shine shoes in the city?

The father made hay while the son shone!

Did you hear about the man who lost his job at the calendar factory because he took a day off?

Did you hear about the man who stole calendars?

He was sentenced to 12 months in jail. They say his days are numbered!

☆

Did you hear about the bicycle that attacked people over and over?

It was a vicious cycle!

☆

Did you hear about the the dating agency for chickens that went out of business?

They couldn't make hens meet!

☆

Did you hear about the man who stayed up all night to see where the sun went?

It finally dawned on him!

Did you hear about the pig's birthday?

They gave a sow-prize party!

Did you hear about the hungry clock?

It went back for seconds!

Did you hear the insect pun?

It really bugs me!

☆

Did you hear about the man who fixed elevators?

His business went up and down!

☆

Did you hear about the florist with two children?

One is a budding genius and the other is a blooming idiot!

☆

Did you hear about the pessimist who is scared of German sausage?

He always fears the wurst!

☆

Did you hear about the statistician?

Probably . . .

☆

Did you hear about the man who was fired from the candle factory?

He refused to work wick-ends!

☆

Did you hear about the rock that was 5,280 feet long?

It was a milestone!

☆

Did you hear about the guy who lost his left arm and leg in a car crash?

He's all right now!

☆

Did you hear about the man who owned the laundry that went out of business?

He was all washed up!

☆

Did you hear about the man who became a vegetarian?

He said it was a big missed steak!

Did you hear about the man who knows sign language?

He finds it handy!

Did you hear about the Spanish magician?

He said uno, dos, and then disappeared without a trace!

Did you hear about the guy who put on a pair of clean socks every day of the week? By Friday he couldn't get his shoes on!

Did you hear that the man who invented the watch has written his autobiography?

It's about time!

☆

Did you hear about the short psychic who broke out of jail?

He was a small medium at large!

☆

Did you hear why the man was fired from the orange juice factory?

He couldn't concentrate!

☆

"Did You Hear?" Jokes

Did you hear about the man who opened a flea circus?

He started it from scratch!

☆

Did you hear about what happened when the past, present, and future went into a bar?

Things got a little tense!

☆

Did you hear about the boy who was named after his father?

They called him Dad!

☆

Did you hear about the young ghost who joined the baseball team?

The coach said they needed a little team spirit!

☆

Did you hear about the man who sold his vacuum cleaner?

It was just collecting dust!

☆

Did you hear about the book that fell on my head?

I only have my-shelf to blame!

☆

Did you hear about the man who had a brain transplant?

He changed his mind!

☆

Did you hear the joke about paper?

It's tearable!

☆

Did you hear about the paranoid bloodhound?

He thought people were following him!

☆

Did you hear about the man who jumped off the bridge in Paris?

He was found in-Seine!

Did you hear about the musical instrument store that was robbed?

The thieves made off with the lute!

Did you hear about the Italian chef?

He pasta way!

Did you hear about the two silk
    worms in a race?

It ended in a tie!

☆

Did you hear about the man who
    plugged his toaster into his
    electric blanket?

He was popping out of bed all night!

☆

Did you hear about the artist who
    was arrested?

He was framed!

☆

Did you hear about the satellite dishes that got married?

The reception was great!

☆

Did you hear about the white board?

It's remarkable!

☆

Did you hear about the guy who couldn't make payments to the exorcist?

He was reposessed!

☆

Did you hear about the cross-eyed lawyer?

He couldn't see eye to eye with his clients!

Did you hear about the new reversible coat?

I want to see how it turns out!

Did you hear that the price of goose feathers has risen?

So now even down is up!

Did you hear about the banana that snored?

He woke up the whole bunch!

☆

Did you hear about the man who died in the sewer?

It was sewer-cide!

☆

Did you hear about the man who attacked me with milk, cream, and butter?

How dairy!

☆

Did you hear the joke about the pizza?

It's really cheesy!

☆

Did you hear about the fire at the circus?

It was in tents!

Did you hear about the race between the lettuce and the tomato?

The lettuce was a "head" and the tomato was trying to "ketchup"!

Did you hear the joke about the roof?

Never mind. It's over your head!

"Knock, Knock" Jokes

Knock, knock!

Who's there?

Theodore!

Theodore who?

Theodore is stuck, please open it!

☆

Knock, knock!

Who's there?

Howard!

Howard who?

Howard I know?

☆

Knock, Knock!

Who's there?

Robin!

Robin who?

Robin you! Hand over your money!

☆

Knock, knock!

Who's there?

Aida!

Aida who?

Aida sandwich for lunch today!

☆

Knock, knock!

Who's there?

Mikey!

Mikey who?

Mikey doesn't work so please unlock the door!

☆

Knock, knock!

Who's there?

Luke!

Luke who?

Luke at me and you'll know!

☆

Knock, knock!

Who's there?

Alice!

Alice who?

Alice fair in love and war!

☆

Knock, knock!

Who's there?

Cher!

Cher who?

Cher would be nice if you'd open the door!

☆

Knock, knock!

Who's there?

Keith!

Keith who?

Keith me my thweetie!

☆

"Knock, Knock" Jokes

Knock, knock!

Who's there?

Dwayne!

Dwayne who?

**Dwayne the bathtub, I'm
dwowning!**

☆

Knock, knock!

Who's there?

Candice!

Candice who?

Candice door open or what?

☆

"Knock, Knock" Jokes

Knock, knock!

Who's there?

Anita!

Anita who?

Anita go to the bathroom!

☆

Knock, knock!

Who's there?

Oswald!

Oswald who?

Oswald my bubble gum!

☆

Knock, knock!

Who's there?

Alec!

Alec who?

Alec it when you ask questions!

☆

Knock, knock!

Who's there?

Ben!

Ben who?

Ben waiting out here a long time!

☆

Knock, knock!

Who's there?

Noah!

Noah who?

Noah good place to get something to eat?

☆

Knock, knock!

Who's there?

Ashe!

Ashe who?

Bless you!

☆

Knock, knock!

Who's there?

Tyrone!

Tyrone who?

Tyrone shoelaces!

☆

Knock, knock!

Who's there?

Jess!

Jess who?

Jess open the door, please!

☆

Knock, knock!

Who's there?

Sam and Janet!

Sam and Janet who?

Sam and Janet evening, you will meet a stranger!

☆

Knock, knock!

Who's there?

Otto!

Otto who?

Otto know. I have amnesia!

☆

"Knock, Knock" Jokes

Knock, knock!

Who's there?

Teresa!

Teresa who?

Teresa green!

☆

Knock, knock!

Who's there?

Aladdin!

Aladdin who?

Aladdin the street wants to talk to
you!

☆

Knock, knock!

Who's there?

Hugh!

Hugh who?

Hugh must be kidding!

☆

Knock, knock!

Who's there?

Alec!

Alec who?

**Alec-tricity can shock you if
you're not careful!**

Knock, knock!

Who's there?

Howell!

Howell who?

**Howell you know unless you open
the door!**

Knock, knock!

Who's there?

Nana!

Nana who?

Nana you're business!

☆

Knock, knock!

Who's there?

Cynthia!

Cynthia who?

Cynthia been away, I've missed you!

☆

Knock, knock!

Who's there?

Henrietta!

Henrietta who?

Henrietta worm in his apple and got sick!

☆

Knock, knock!

Who's there?

Omar!

Omar who?

Omar goodness gracious it's good to see you!

☆

Knock, knock!

Who's there?

Alfred!

Alfred who?

Alfred of the dark!

☆

"Knock, Knock" Jokes

Knock, knock!

Who's there?

Aaron!

Aaron who?

Aaron the side of caution!

☆

Knock, knock!

Who's there?

Justin!

Justin who?

Justin the neighborhood, mind if I
come in?

☆

Knock, knock!

Who's there?

Colleen!

Colleen who?

Colleen up this mess!

☆

Knock, knock!

Who's there?

Dewey!

Dewey who?

Dewey have to go to school today?

☆

Knock, knock!

Who's there?

Lief!

Lief who?

Lief me alone!

☆

Knock, knock!

Who's there?

Mary!

Mary who?

Mary Christmas!

Knock, knock!

Who's there?

Annie!

Annie who?

Annie way you can open the door for me?

Knock, knock!

Who's there?

Gladys!

Gladys who?

Gladys the weekend, no school!

Knock, knock!

Who's there?

Doris!

Doris who?

Doris locked. Open it up!

Knock, knock!

Who's there?

Maia!

Maia who?

Maia-bilities are too great for these stupid jokes!

Knock, knock!

Who's there?

Abe!

Abe who?

Abe C D E F G . . .

Knock, knock!

Who's there?

Amos!

Amos who?

Amos-quito!

Knock, knock!

Who's there?

Alison!

Alice who?

Alison to music in the car!

☆

Knock, knock!

Who's there?

Ken!

Ken who?

Ken I come in, I'm cold!

☆

"Knock, Knock" Jokes

Knock, knock!

Who's there?

June!

June who?

June know how long I've been knocking on your door?

Knock, knock!

Who's there?

Claire!

Claire who?

Claire the way, I'm coming through!

"Knock, Knock" Jokes

Knock, knock!

Who's there?

Art!

Art who?

R2-D2!

☆

Knock, knock!

Who's there?

Olive!

Olive who?

Olive you very much!

☆

Knock, knock!

Who's there?

Ariel!

Ariel who?

**Ariel live nephew of my Uncle
Sam!**

☆

"Knock, Knock" Jokes

Knock, knock!

Who's there?

Carmen!

Carmen who?

Carmen get it while it's hot!

Knock, knock!

Who's there?

Annie!

Annie who?

Annie thing you can do, I can do better!

Knock, knock!

Who's there?

Euripides!

Euripides who?

Euripides pants, you're going to have to buy a new pair!

Knock, knock!

Who's there?

Oscar!

Oscar who?

Oscar silly question, get a silly answer!

☆

Knock, knock!

Who's there?

Alex!

Alex who?

Alex plain when you open the door!

☆

Knock, knock!

Who's there?

Conrad!

Conrad who?

Conrad-ulations! You just won a prize!

☆

"Knock, Knock" Jokes

Knock, knock!

Who's there?

Kanye!

Kanye who?

Kanye come out and play?

Knock, knock!

Who's there?

Heidi!

Heidi who?

Heidi who, Heidi ho neighbor!

Knock, knock!

Who's there?

Lena!

Lena who?

**Lena little closer and I'll tell you
another joke!**